CAKES

Cook Books from Amish Kitchens

Phyllis Pellman Good • Rachel Thomas Pellman

Good Books

Intercourse, PA 17534
800/762-7171
www.GoodBks.com

CAKES

Cook Books from Amish Kitchens

Eat a banana or eggs with warm shoo-fly cake and you have a breakfast. Dollop the cake with whipped cream and you have dessert.

Sometimes cakes turn up at breakfast, in lunch boxes, and at company dinners. Cakes are treats, but then they're also part of daily fare. The special part.

Cover art and design by Cheryl A. Benner.
Design and art in body by Craig N. Heisey; Calligraphy by Gayle Smoker.
This special edition is an adaptation of *Cakes: From Amish and Mennonite Kitchens, Pennsylvania Dutch Cookbook*
Copyright © 1983, 1991, 1996 by Good Books, Intercourse, PA 17534. ISBN-10: 1-56148-197-1.
ISBN-13: 978-1-56148-197-2. All rights reserved. Printed in the United States of America.

Contents

Moist Chocolate Cake

2 cups flour, sifted
2 cups sugar
¾ cup cocoa
2 tsp. baking soda
1 tsp. baking powder
pinch salt
½ cup oil
1 cup hot coffee
1 cup milk
2 eggs

1. Mix together flour, sugar, cocoa, baking soda and powder, and salt.
2. Make a well in the center of the dry ingredients and add oil, coffee, milk, and eggs. Beat just enough to mix well. (Batter will be lumpy.)

3. Pour into a greased 9"x 13" cake pan and bake 35 minutes at 350°.
4. Spread slightly warm cake with Quick Carmel Frosting (or any other favorite!).

Mother Pellman's Chocolate Cake

1½ cups sugar
½ cup vegetable oil
   or margarine
2 eggs
½ cup sour milk or buttermilk
3 heaping Tbsp. cocoa (scant ½ cup)
1 cup boiling water
2½ cups all-purpose flour, sifted
2 tsp. baking powder
1 tsp. baking soda
¼ tsp. salt
1 tsp. vanilla

Makes 1 layer or
1 long cake

1. Cream the sugar and shortening together until lemon-colored. Then beat in eggs and sour milk or buttermilk.
2. Pour boiling water over cocoa and stir until it thickens slightly. Add to the creamed mixture.
3. Add flour, baking powder, soda, salt, and vanilla and beat well.
4. Pour into a greased and floured 9"x 13" pan or two 9" layer pans. Bake 20-25 minutes at 350°.

Chocolate Cake Roll

3 eggs, separated   Makes 10~12 servings
1 cup sugar
⅓ cup water
1 cup flour
1 tsp. baking powder
confectioner's sugar
2 Tbsp. cocoa
2 Tbsp. cornstarch
¾ cup sugar
1 cup cold water
1 Tbsp. butter or margarine
½ tsp. vanilla

1. Beat 3 egg yolks, 1 cup sugar, and water together until light. Slowly beat in flour and baking powder.
2. Beat 3 egg whites until stiff peaks form. Fold flour and egg mixture carefully into beaten whites.
3. Pour into greased and floured jelly roll pan. Bake at 425° for 8 minutes.
4. Loosen hot cake from sides of pan and invert on a cotton towel dusted with confect~ioner's sugar. While cake is still hot, roll up in the towel for a few minutes, then unroll.
5. Stir cocoa, cornstarch, sugar, and water

together in a saucepan. Heat until mixture comes to a boil.

6. Remove from heat. Stir in butter and vanilla. Cool. Then spread on cake. Roll cake, slice (¼" slices) and serve. Sprinkle with confectioner's sugar, if desired, before serving.

Quick Carmel Frosting

½ cup butter or margarine
1 cup brown sugar
¼ cup milk
1¾-2 cups sifted confectioner's sugar

1. Melt butter in saucepan. Add brown sugar and cook over low heat two minutes, stirring constantly.
2. Add milk and continue stirring until mixture comes to a boil.
3. Remove from heat and cool. Add confectioner's sugar until frosting reaches spreading consistency.

"Lovelight" Chocolate Chiffon Cake

2 eggs, separated
1½ cups sugar
1¾ cups cake flour, sifted
¾ tsp. baking soda
¾ tsp. salt
4 Tbsp. cocoa
⅓ cup vegetable oil
1 cup buttermilk

Makes 1 layer or long cake

1. Beat egg whites until frothy. Gradually add ½ cup sugar. Beat mixture until very stiff. Set aside.
2. Sift remaining sugar, flour, soda, salt, and cocoa into another bowl. Add oil and half of buttermilk. Beat 1 minute with mixer.
3. Add remaining buttermilk and egg yolks and beat one more minute. Fold in egg white mixture.
4. Pour into 2 greased and floured 8" round cake pans or 1 9"x 13" baking pan. Bake at 350° for 35~40 minutes.

Chocolate Angel Food Cake

1¼ cups egg whites   Makes 1 tube cake
¼ tsp. salt
1 tsp. cream of tartar
1¼ cups granulated sugar, sifted
¾ cup cake flour, sifted
4 Tbsp. cocoa
1 tsp. vanilla

1. Beat egg whites, salt, and cream of tartar until the whites mixture stands in peaks.
2. Gradually fold in sugar.
3. Fold in very gradually, a tablespoon or two at a time, the sifted flour and cocoa mixture. Then gently add the vanilla.
4. When well blended, pour into an ungreased tube pan and bake at 275° for 30 minutes, then increase temperature to 325° and bake for 30~45 minutes longer.

Party Angel Food Cake

1 cup and 2 Tbsp.   Makes 1 tube cake
    cake flour, sifted
¾ cup sugar
1⅔ cups egg whites (about 12)
1½ tsp. cream of tartar
½ tsp. salt
1 tsp. vanilla
½ tsp. almond flavoring
¾ cup sugar
½ cup pecans, chopped

1. Sift the flour and ¾ cup sugar together four times. Set aside.
2. Combine egg whites, cream of tartar, salt, vanilla, and almond flavoring and beat until the whites are stiff but not dry.
3. Add ¾ cup sugar, 2 tablespoons at a time, folding it in well each time.
4. Then add flour~sugar mixture in four parts, folding in the additions with 15 strokes each time.
5. Finally, fold in the pecans.
6. Pour into an ungreased 10" tube pan; then gently draw a thin spatula through the batter to break any large air bubbles. Bake at 350° for 45 minutes. Invert and cool.

Shoo-Fly Cake

    4 cups flour (use 2   Makes 1 long cake
      cups whole wheat flour and 2 cups
      white flour if desired)
    2 cups brown sugar
    1 cup butter or margarine
    2 cups boiling water
    1 cup molasses
    2 tsp. baking soda

1. Work the flour, sugar, and butter into fine crumbs with your fingers or a pastry mixer. Set aside 1½ cups crumbs for topping.
2. Mix water, molasses, and baking soda together. Then add to the remaining crumbs. Mix until batter is very thin yet still lumpy.
3. Pour into greased and floured 9"x 13" cake pan. Sprinkle with reserved crumbs. Bake at 350° for 35 minutes.

"Best served slightly warm, fresh from the oven."

Hot Milk Sponge Cake

2 cups cake flour Makes 1 long cake
2 tsp. baking powder
½ tsp. salt
4 eggs
2 tsp. vanilla
2 cups granulated sugar
1 cup milk
2 Tbsp. butter

1. Sift flour, baking powder, and salt together.
2. Beat eggs and vanilla together; then gradually add sugar and continue beating until mixture becomes light and lemon colored.
3. Blend dry ingredients into creamed mixture.
4. Bring milk and butter to the boiling point; then quickly stir into batter. Blend well.
5. Pour quickly into a 13"x 9"x 2" baking pan which has been greased and floured on the bottom only. Bake at 350° for 35-40 minutes.

Variations:
1. Add ½ tsp. almond extract to the egg and vanilla mixture.
2. Add 1 tsp. lemon flavoring and 1 tsp. orange flavoring to the egg and vanilla mixture.

Short Cake

2 cups flour   Makes 4-6 servings
2 Tbsp. sugar
½ tsp. salt
2½ tsp. baking powder
4 Tbsp. margarine
1 cup milk

1. Stir dry ingredients together; then cut in margarine.
2. Add milk and mix well until batter is quite stiff.
3. Spread batter in round cake pan or on a cookie sheet, about ¾" thick.
4. Bake at 325° until golden in color, but not brown.

Chiffon Cake

2 cups cake flour,   Makes 1 tube pan cake
     sifted
1½ cups sugar
3 tsp. baking powder
1 tsp. salt
½ cup vegetable oil
7 egg yolks, unbeaten
¾ cup cold water
2 tsp. vanilla
2 tsp. lemon rind, grated
½ tsp. cream of tartar
7 egg whites

1. Sift flour, sugar, baking powder, and salt together two or three times.
2. Mix oil, egg yolks, water, vanilla, and lemon rind together well; then add to the dry ingredients and blend until smooth.
3. Add cream of tartar to egg whites; then beat until very stiff, but not dry.
4. Pour the creamed mixture in a thin stream over the egg whites; then fold gently together until well blended.
5. Pour into an ungreased tube pan. Bake at 325° for 65 minutes. Turn off oven, but do not remove cake for another 5

minutes.

6. Remove cake from oven and invert pan until cake cools.

Variation:
   Add 1 tsp. cinnamon, ½ tsp. ground cloves, ½ tsp. nutmeg and a dash of allspice to the dry ingredients before sifting.

Crumb Cake

3 cups flour   Makes 1 long cake
2 cups brown sugar
½ cup shortening, butter or margarine
1 egg, beaten
1 cup buttermilk
1 tsp. baking soda
1 tsp. cream of tarter

1. Mix flour and brown sugar together. Cut in shortening until mixture is crumbly. Take out 1 cup crumbs for topping.
2. Add to remaining crumbs, the next 4 ingredients in the order they are listed. Mix well after each addition.
3. Pour into a greased 9"x13" baking pan. Sprinkle reserved cup of crumbs over top. Bake at 375° for 25~30 minutes.

Pumpkin Chiffon Cake

2 cups cake flour,   Makes 1 tube pan cake
    sifted
1½ cups sugar
3 tsp. baking powder
1 tsp. cinnamon
½ tsp. ground nutmeg
½ tsp. ground cloves
½ cup vegetable oil
8 egg yolks
½ cup water
¾ cup canned or cooked mashed pumpkin
½ tsp. cream of tartar
8 egg whites

1. Sift all dry ingredients into a large mixing bowl.
2. Make a deep well in the center. Add, in order, salad oil, egg yolks, water, and pumpkin. Beat until satiny smooth.
3. Add the cream of tartar to the egg whites. Beat until very stiff, but not dry.
4. Pour the pumpkin mixture in a thin stream over the egg whites; then gently fold into the whites with a spatula.
5. Bake in an ungreased tube pan 55 minutes at 325°. Then increase heat to

350° and bake 10 more minutes.
6. Invert pan until cake cools. Remove from pan and cover with maple frosting and nuts.

Cream Cheese Frosting
   4 Tbsp. butter or margarine, softened
   3 oz. package Philadelphia cream cheese, softened
   2 cups confectioner's sugar
   1 tsp. vanilla

1. Beat together until smooth.
2. Spread on slightly warm cake.

Quick Sugar and Cinnamon Coffee Cake

1½ cups cake flour,   Makes 1 square cake
    sifted
¼ tsp. salt
2 tsp. baking powder
⅔ cup sugar
¼ cup shortening, melted
1 egg
½ cup milk
½ tsp. vanilla

1. Sift dry ingredients together. Add remaining ingredients.
2. Beat altogether in electric mixer on number 3 speed, about 2 minutes. Scrape sides and bottom of bowl while beating.
3. Pour batter into 8" square baking pan or a deep 9" layer cake pan. Bake at 350° for 25 minutes. Remove from oven and put on Topping.

Topping

4 Tbsp. butter or margarine, melted
¼ cup sugar
½ tsp. cinnamon

1. Brush warm cake with butter.
2. Mix sugar and cinnamon together. Sprinkle over top.
3. Return cake to oven and bake 5 minutes longer.

Black Walnut Cake

¾ cup shortening
1¼ cups brown sugar
3 eggs
1½ cups buttermilk
2¾ cups flour
1⅓ tsp. baking soda
½ tsp. allspice
1 tsp. salt
1 cup black walnuts, chopped

Makes 1 layer or
1 long cake

1. Cream shortening and sugar together. Add eggs and beat until lemon-colored.
2. Sift together dry ingredients. Add them alternately with the buttermilk to the creamed mixture, beating well after each addition.
3. Stir in the walnuts.
4. Pour batter into greased 9"x 13" pan or two 9" round layer pans. Bake 35~40 minutes at 350°.

German Apple Cake

½ cup shortening   Makes 1 long cake
1 cup sugar
½ cup brown sugar
2 eggs
2¼ cups flour
2 tsp. cinnamon
2 tsp. baking soda
1 cup sour milk
2 cups raw apples, peeled and diced

1. Beat shortening until smooth. Add sugars and eggs and beat until fluffy.
2. Mix flour and cinnamon together. Combine soda and sour milk. Then add the dry ingredients and the milk alternately to the creamed mixture.
3. When well blended, fold in apples.
4. Pour into greased 9"x 13" cake pan. Sprinkle topping over cake and then bake at 350° for 45-50 minutes.

Topping

½ cup brown sugar
¼ cup sugar
½ tsp. cinnamon
½ cup chopped nuts or coconut

Hannah's Raisin Cake

2 cups boiling water   Makes 1 layer or
1 lb. raisins   tube cake
½ cup shortening
2 cups sugar
1 cup buttermilk or sour milk
½ tsp. salt
1 tsp. cinnamon
½ tsp. cloves
1 Tbsp. baking soda
4 cups flour

1. Pour boiling water over raisins in sauce pan. Boil 15 minutes. Let cool.
2. Cream shortening and sugar together. Add buttermilk.
3. Combine all dry ingredients; then add to creamy mixture. When well blended, stir in raisins.
4. Bake at 350° for 30-45 minutes in either 2 layer pans or a tube pan.

Raw Apple Cake

1 cup sugar

Makes 1 long cake

1 cup vegetable oil

3 eggs

1 tsp. vanilla

1½ cups flour

½ cup whole wheat flour

1 tsp. cinnamon

1 tsp. soda

1 tsp. salt

5 cups raw apples, diced

½ cup nuts, chopped

½ tsp. cinnamon

¼ cup sugar

1. Blend first 4 ingredients together in mixing bowl. Add the next 5 ingredients and stir well.
2. Fold in the apples and nuts.
3. Spread batter in greased 9" x 13" baking pan.
4. Mix together cinnamon and sugar and sprinkle over batter.
5. Bake at 350° for 45 minutes.

Blueberry Cake

¾ cup sugar
¼ cup vegetable oil
1 egg
½ cup milk
2 cups flour
2 tsp. baking powder
½ tsp. salt
2 cups blueberries, well drained

Makes 9~12 servings

1.   Cream together the sugar, oil, and egg until lemon-colored. Stir in milk, thoroughly.
2.   Sift together the flour, baking powder, and salt and stir into creamed mixture.
3.   Gently fold in the blueberries.
4.   Spread batter into a greased and floured 9"x 9" square baking pan. Sprinkle with topping.   Bake 45~50 minutes at 375°. Serve warm.

Topping

¼ cup butter or margarine
½ cup granulated sugar
⅓ cup flour
½ tsp. cinnamon

1. Melt butter. Stir in sugar, flour, and cinnamon.
2. Crumble over cake batter.

Carrot Cake

3 eggs   Makes 1 long cake
2 cups flour, sifted
2 cups sugar
1¼ cups vegetable oil
2 tsp. baking soda
1 tsp. cinnamon
1 tsp. salt
2 tsp. vanilla
1 cup shredded coconut
1 cup walnuts, chopped
1 cup crushed pineapple, drained
2 cups raw carrot, shredded

1. Beat eggs well; then add the next seven ingredients and beat well until smooth.
2. Stir in the coconut, nuts, pineapple, and carrots with a mixing spoon.
3. Pour into a greased 9"x 13" cake pan and bake at 350° for 50 minutes.
4. When cake is slightly warm, spread with Cream Cheese Frosting. (page 17)

Pumpkin Cake

4 eggs, well beaten
2 cups sugar
1½ cups vegetable oil
3 cups flour
3 tsp. baking powder
2 tsp. cinnamon
2 tsp. baking soda
¼ tsp. salt
½ tsp. ginger
2 cups pumpkin
1 cup walnuts, chopped

Makes 1 layer or
long cake

1. To the beaten eggs add the sugar and blend well. Beat in oil.
2. Add the dry ingredients and pumpkin and mix thoroughly. Stir in walnuts by hand.
3. Pour batter into well greased and floured 9"x 13" baking pan or 2 round 9" pans. Bake at 350° for 45-60 minutes (test center with pick to be sure cake is fully baked).
4. Frost with Cream Cheese Icing on page 17.

Zucchini Squash Cake

4 eggs   Makes 1 tube cake
2 cups sugar
1 cup vegetable oil
2 cups flour
2 tsp. cinnamon
2 tsp. baking powder
1 tsp. baking soda
1 tsp. salt
1 can (8¼ oz.) crushed pineapple,
    well drained
1 cup walnuts, chopped
2 cups grated raw (or frozen) unpeeled
    zucchini squash
2 tsp. vanilla

1.   In a large mixing bowl beat the eggs and sugar together until lemon-colored. Add vegetable oil and beat until well blended.
2.   In a separate bowl sift together the flour, cinnamon, baking powder, baking soda, and salt. Add dry ingredients to creamed mixture and beat two minutes.
3.   Stir in pineapple, walnuts, zucchini (squeeze in a paper towel to remove excess moisture), and vanilla. Mix thoroughly.

4. Pour batter into a well greased and floured 10" tube pan. Bake at 350° for 1 hour and 20 minutes. Cool on rack for 30 minutes and remove from pan.
5. Glaze cake, if desired, with 1 cup confectioner's sugar mixed with 1 Tbsp. milk.

Banana Cake

4 cups ripe banana, cut fine   Makes 1 long cake

2 eggs, beaten
1½ cups sugar
½ cup oil
1 tsp. vanilla
½ cup nuts, chopped
2 cups flour
2 tsp. baking soda
1 tsp. salt

1. Cream banana, eggs, sugar, oil, and vanilla together until smooth. Stir in nuts.
2. Sift together flour, baking soda, and salt.
3. Add dry ingredients to creamed mixture, blending just until all ingredients are moistened. Do not over mix.
4. Bake at 350° for 40~45 minutes in a 9"x 13" pan.

Hot Applesauce Cake

½ cup shortening   Makes 1 loaf cake
1⅓ cups sugar
2 eggs
2 cups flour
1 tsp. cinnamon
½ tsp. nutmeg
¼ tsp. ground cloves
1 cup hot applesauce
1 tsp. baking soda dissolved in
    2 Tbsp. hot water
1 cup raisins
⅓ cup walnuts, chopped

1. Cream shortening and sugar together until fluffy. Blend eggs in thoroughly.
2. Sift dry ingredients together. Add them alternately with the hot applesauce to the creamed mixture. Beat well after each addition.
3. Add soda dissolved in water and mix well.
4. Flour raisins and nuts lightly and fold into mixture.
5. Bake in a greased 5"x 9"x 4" loaf pan at 350° for 1 hour and 10 minutes, or until firm in the middle when tested with a toothpick.

Mandarin Orange Cake

2 eggs   Makes 1 long cake
2 11 oz. cans mandarin oranges,
     well drained
2 cups flour
2 cups sugar
2 tsp. baking soda
½ tsp. salt

1. Beat eggs. Add oranges and dry ingredients. Beat 4 minutes with electric mixer on slow speed until oranges flake through the batter. Pour into greased 9"x13" cake pan.
2. Bake at 350° for 35-40 minutes. Cake will get quite dark. Before removing from oven, press top with finger tip to see if it bounces back. If it doesn't, bake a bit longer, taking care that it doesn't burn.
3. Remove cake from oven. Pour topping over. Return cake to oven and bake 5 minutes longer.

Topping

¾ cup brown sugar
3 Tbsp. milk
2 Tbsp. butter or margarine

Combine and bring to a rolling boil.

Oatmeal Cake

1¼ cups boiling water

Makes 1 long cake

1 cup oatmeal

½ cup margarine, softened

1 cup brown sugar

1 cup granulated sugar

2 eggs

1½ cups flour

1 tsp. baking soda

2 tsp. baking powder

1 tsp. cinnamon

1 tsp. salt

1. Pour boiling water over oatmeal. Set aside.
2. Cream together margarine, sugars, and eggs. Then add oatmeal mixture and the remaining ingredients.
3. Pour batter into a greased 9"x13" baking pan and bake at 350° for 30 minutes.
4. Cool cake and spread with Topping (page 31). Put under broiler until topping bubbles, about 2 minutes.

Out-of-This-World Cake

    2 cups sugar   Makes 1 loaf cake
    ½ lb. butter or margarine, softened
    4 eggs
    1 cup milk
    2 tsp. baking powder
    3⅓ cups graham cracker crumbs
    1 cup coconut
    1 cup nuts
    1 20 oz. can crushed pineapple   drained

1. Beat first 6 ingredients together well. Then fold in the coconut, nuts, and pineapple.
2. Pour into a greased 9"x13" baking pan and bake at 350° for 1 hour.

Topping

    ¼ cup butter or margarine, softened
    ⅔ cup brown sugar
    ¼ cup milk
    1 cup coconut
    1 cup pecans, chopped

    Mix together and spread on cake. Return cake to oven and bake 5 minutes or until topping bubbles and is slightly browned.

Spice Cake

2 cups brown sugar	Makes 1 layer cake
½ cup butter	or 1 long cake
2 eggs	
1 cup sour milk	
2½ cups sifted flour	
1½ tsp. baking powder	
1 tsp. cinnamon	
1 tsp. nutmeg	
1 tsp. baking soda	
1 tsp. vanilla	

1. Cream sugar and butter together until fluffy.
2. Add eggs and beat until light.
3. Sift together all dry ingredients; then add them alternately with the milk to the creamed mixture, beating well after each addition. Then mix in the vanilla.
4. Pour into greased layer pans or a 9" x 13" cake pan. Bake at 350° for 35-40 minutes.